Byang Kato

by Simonetta Carr

with Illustrations by Matt Abraxas

REFORMATION HERITAGE BOOKS

Grand Rapids, Michigan

Byang Kato
© 2022 by Simonetta Carr

Cover artwork by Matt Abraxas
For additional artwork by Matt, see pages 9, 11, 15, 19, 27, 31, 35, 41, 43, 45, 51, and 53.

Reformation Heritage Books
3070 29th St. SE
Grand Rapids, MI 49512
616-977-0889
orders@heritagebooks.org
www.heritagebooks.org

Printed in the United States of America
22 23 24 25 26/10 9 8 7 6 5 4 3 2 1

Library of Congress Cataloging-in-Publication Data

Names: Carr, Simonetta, author. | Abraxas, Matt, illustrator.
Title: Byang Kato / by Simonetta Carr ; with illustrations by Matt Abraxas.
Description: Grand Rapids, Michigan : Reformation Heritage Books, [2022] |
    Series: Christian biographies for young readers | Audience: Ages 7 to 12
Identifiers: LCCN 2022004561 | ISBN 9781601789259 (hardcover)
Subjects: LCSH: Kato, Byang H.—Juvenile literature. | Theologians—Nigeria—
    Biography—Juvenile literature. | Evangelical Churches of West Africa—
    Biography—Juvenile literature. | BISAC: JUVENILE NONFICTION /
    Biography & Autobiography / Historical
Classification: LCC BX4827.K327 C37 2022 |
    DDC 230.0966—dc23/eng/20220215
LC record available at https://lccn.loc.gov/2022004561

For additional Reformed literature, request a free book list from Reformation Heritage Books at the above regular or email address.

CHRISTIAN BIOGRAPHIES FOR YOUNG READERS

This series introduces children to important people in the Christian tradition. Parents and schoolteachers alike will welcome the excellent educational value it provides for students, while the quality of the publication and the artwork make each volume a keepsake for generations to come. Furthermore, the books in the series go beyond the simple story of someone's life by teaching young readers the historical and theological relevance of each character.

AVAILABLE VOLUMES OF THE SERIES

John Calvin	Martin Luther
Augustine of Hippo	Peter Martyr Vermigli
John Owen	Irenaeus
Athanasius	John Newton
Lady Jane Grey	Julia Gonzaga
Anselm of Canterbury	B.B. Warfield
John Knox	John Bunyan
Jonathan Edwards	Phillis Wheatley
Marie Durand	Charles Haddon Spurgeon

Table of Contents

Introduction 5

Chapter 1: Entering the Boat of Salvation 6

Chapter 2: More Than a Shirt 13

Chapter 3: Student and Leader 22

Chapter 4: For the African Church 33

Chapter 5: Leaving a Powerful Message 52

Time Line of Kato's Life 57

Did You Know? 58

From the Pen of Byang Kato 62

Acknowledgments 64

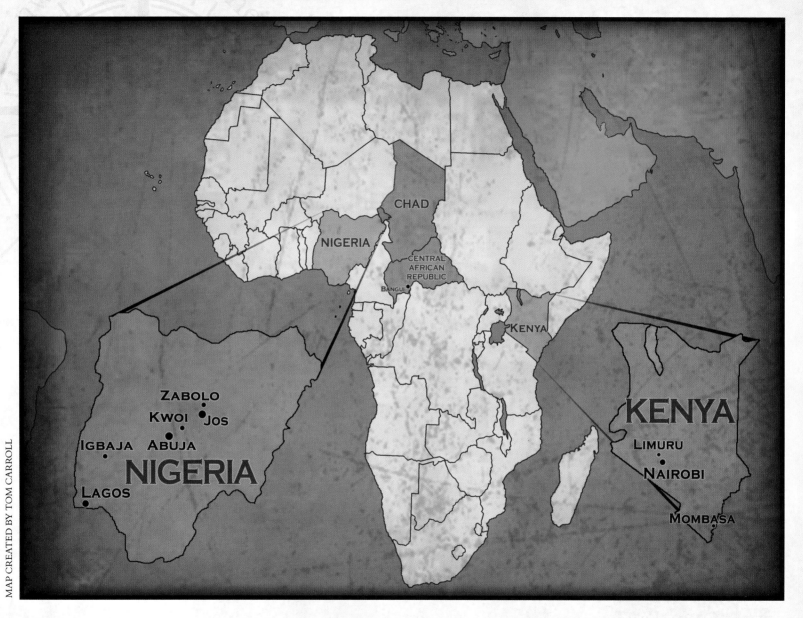

MAP CREATED BY TOM CARROLL

A map of Africa during Byang Kato's life

Introduction

Byang Kato (pronounced bee-ahng kah-toh) lived in Africa at a time when many nations were declaring their independence from the European countries that had ruled them. Seventeen African nations became independent in 1960 alone, the so-called African year, when Kato was twenty-four.

This independence brought hope, excitement, and challenges as each nation tried to set up the best government for its needs and culture. At the same time, African churches learned to become more independent of European help. Some Africans wondered if Christianity in Africa should look different than it did in other parts of the world. If so, how?

COURTESY OF DALLAS THEOLOGICAL SEMINARY

Byang Kato in 1970

As African Christians tried to answer these questions, Byang Kato reminded them to always keep in mind what Christianity meant and who they were in Christ. He lived a short life, but his writings have continued to bring changes and encouragement in Africa and, as they are discovered, around the world.

CHAPTER ONE
Entering the Boat of Salvation

Byang Kato was born on June 23, 1936, in Sabzuro, in the district of Kwoi, in the Kaduna State of northern Nigeria. At that time Kwoi had about fifteen thousand people. The people in that area are often known as Jaba but refer to themselves as Ham.

Byang's parents, Hari and Zawi, followed the traditional juju religion of Nigeria and Ghana, which included the use of objects and words people believed had magical powers. Juju worship required bloody sacrifices (sometimes of human beings) and torture. Later in life, Byang noticed that juju worshipers learned to be hardhearted and cruel, especially against those who opposed them.

Countryside near
Kwoi, Nigeria
IRENE BECKER

Hari and Zawi were devoted to their religion and wanted their firstborn son to become a juju priest. In fact, when six of their next seven children died as babies, the family saw it as confirmation that juju was protecting Byang above all the others. "I was dedicated to serve the devil as a baby," Byang wrote later. "I know now it was really God who was protecting me, because He had a purpose for my life."

Hari taught Byang to offer sacrifices to the gods. Every year, before they could eat any of the products of the earth, Hari and Byang placed the first portion of the harvest at the base of a sycamore tree where people thought the spirits lived. Then, when Byang was ten, his parents sent him to the nearby forest for the traditional one-week initiation.

Byang Kato as a child
PAUL KATO

Initiations were special events that marked the transition of boys from children to men. The boys were made to live in harsh and often dangerous conditions. They usually spent each day in a large cave. At night they walked around special areas of the forest that were devoted to the spirits. There they were taught lessons and secrets about the juju, a spiritual power that was "bigger than two houses put together, and present everywhere." There were tests, and those who failed received terrible beatings.

The local people believed that during this time of initiation the boys were in the "stomach" of the juju. For this reason, the boys' mothers went to the forest daily to offer good food and drinks to the juju so that it could be filled and vomit out their sons. The boys were allowed to eat the food, but only after the juju leaders had mixed it with dirt.

A forest near Kwoi
IRENE BECKER

The boys spent the day in a large cave and walked around special areas of the forest at night.

Byang passed the initiation with flying colors. That meant he was considered a man and could join the men in their activities. He also qualified to become a juju priest. He was looking forward to wearing the special priestly clothes and eating all the good food that juju worshipers brought during their worship.

At the same time, the gospel of Jesus Christ was being preached everywhere in Nigeria, and many people were becoming Christian. Half of the population in the region where Byang lived had already converted.

One day a teacher from the nearby Christian mission, Mary Haas, visted Kato's village. She brought a phonograph (an old-fashioned version of a CD player) and set it by a rock in the center of town. She then used it to play songs and Bible stories in the Hausa language of that region. Byang was fascinated by what he called the "black box." He thought there were people singing and talking inside. Every time Haas returned to town, Byang was there.

Byang was fascinated by the phonograph, which played songs and
Bible stories, and wished he could see the people inside.

Byang Kato as a child
PAUL KATO

One of Byang's friends was a Christian who attended a school in Kwoi sponsored by the Sudan Interior Mission. Byang asked if he could come along and was surprised when his friend encouraged him to. The boys also attended Sunday school, where Byang heard more Bible stories.

When Byang first heard the story about Noah and the flood, he understood that God was calling him to enter the "boat of salvation," just like He called Noah and his family to enter the ark. Byang accepted the teacher's invitation to pray to Jesus as his Savior, even though he didn't fully understand everything that prayer meant.

At first Byang's parents didn't pay much attention to his new interests, but when church and school started to interfere with his work on the family's farm, his father refused to let him go. "You want to be lazy like some of the other boys who have been spoiled by going to school!" Hari said.

CHAPTER TWO
More Than a Shirt

Obeying his father, Byang didn't go back to the mission for over a year. Finally, the church elders and another teacher talked with Hari. After a few visits, Hari agreed to let Byang attend the school every afternoon, after a morning of work on the farm. But he was not going to pay for any school fees, so Byang worked part-time at the school in the evenings. This taught Byang to make the most of his time. By studying hard, he ranked first in his class.

On November 21, 1948, after Byang had learned more about Jesus, the local pastor, Raymond Veenker, baptized him together with about three hundred other people. Pastor Veenker gave Byang a new name, Henry, which he kept as his middle name.

A farmer harvesting rice near Kwoi
IRENE BECKER

As he continued to grow and study, Byang started to teach Sunday school and became involved in Christian organizations such as the Boys' Brigade and Youth for Christ. Later, however, he confessed that his life had not fully changed, and his lifestyle seemed to contradict what he was saying.

All this began to change in 1953 when two visiting pastors spoke at his church for a week. "The Holy Spirit convicted us of our selfishness," Byang wrote. "Nearly a thousand men and women wept for their sins….With my heart breaking within me, and tears streaming down my face, I went forward to confess my sins before the Lord and His people."

To show his thankfulness for God's forgiveness, Byang took off his shirt and laid it next to the offerings of clothes, money, goats, and grain that other people were making. It was a huge gift because it was the better of the two shirts he owned. But as he knelt to pray, he understood that Jesus didn't really want his shirt; He wanted Byang's life. "Lord, I give You my life," Byang said. "I don't know what You want me to be, but I dedicate myself to You. Do whatever You want with me." He was seventeen years old.

Byang took off his shirt and laid it next to the other gifts to the church.

This was an important moment in his life. He immediately started to teach neighborhood children who could not afford to attend school. He also became convinced that he should go to a Bible college. His friends teased him, calling him "pastor," "bishop," or even "pope." Most people didn't understand why he didn't choose a career that would give him more money, especially since he was the top student in his school.

The hostel where Kato lived as a student
COURTESY OF REV. STEPHEN OLUWAROTIMI Y. BABA

"There were many obstacles in the way," he later wrote, "the scorn of family and friends, lack of money, and my own fears and doubts. But when I fully yielded to the Lord, everything worked out."

The mission suggested that he attend a Bible college in Igbaja, about three hundred miles south of Kwoi. At first Byang didn't even know how he would pay for the train ticket, let alone the school's fees. But he made arrangements anyway. In 1955, one week before his scheduled departure, he received a letter without a return address that included exactly enough money for the train. Soon after that, his pastor told him the church had agreed to pay for his school fees for the first year.

In Igbaja Byang began to think about marriage. After some time of thought and prayer, he realized the best wife for him was a young woman he had known since they were children: Jummai (pronounced jummah) Rahila. Unlike Byang, Jummai had been raised a Christian from a young age by her grandmother Lydia, who taught her family the Bible every morning and evening.

Byang and Jummai had first met at the mission school in Kwoi. On their way home, Byang used to stop at Jummai's house, where her family would offer him a cold drink. The two stayed friends and wrote to each other when Byang was in college.

Igbaja Bible College (now ECWA Theological Seminary, Igbaja), in the Kwara State of Nigeria

COURTESY OF REV. STEPHEN OLUWAROTIMI Y. BABA

"I've prayed a long time to know the Lord's choice for my wife," Byang told Jummai in a letter. "I'm certain you are the one." Jummai accepted his proposal, and the two married in Kwoi in January 1957 during Byang's winter break. She was two years younger than he was.

After the wedding the couple traveled back to Igbaja, where Byang continued his studies. He also taught a few classes, sang in a quartet, and helped to publish the school's magazine. Jummai spent most of her days at home because she didn't speak the language of that region, Yoruba. Ten months after their wedding, the couple had their first baby, Deborah Bosede, and Jummai started to make friends with other mothers in the community.

Byang graduated from Bible college in December 1957. Then he and Jummai returned to Kwoi, where he taught at the local Bible school. He also stayed active in the local church and worked with Christian organizations for young people. Full of energy and new ideas, he created games and activities and organized a choir and a church newspaper. On Fridays he took young Christians to the local market, where they took turns standing on a chair and telling others about Jesus.

Byang took a group of young people to the local market to tell others about Jesus.

For the first year, however, the school paid Byang only fifteen dollars a month (the equivalent of about 150 dollars today), hardly enough for a growing family, so he had to do some farming on the side. Jummai's family also helped with some basic food items, such as corn, palm oil, and salt.

"There were times when we had to eat only sweet potatoes," Byang wrote. There were also "times when I did not know what my family would eat the next day, but the Lord always provided when the time came" and "gave us peace and satisfaction in serving Him."

Eventually, the school started to pay him a little more. But he also received an invitation to work for a Christian magazine called *African Challenge* that was based in Lagos, the largest city in Nigeria. The magazine received almost two thousand letters a month from people who had questions about God and needed someone who could provide biblical answers. Byang accepted.

The River Medway near
Maidstone, Kent
LUKE MCKERNAN

Moving to a large, busy city was a big change for the Kato family, who had just grown to include a baby boy, Jonathan Nzuno. Byang was especially impressed by the ocean, which he had never seen before. "Even if I should die now," he said, "I thank God I have seen the sea."

From the start Byang left a great impression on the newspaper editor, Harold Fuller. "A man of twenty-three is considered a youth in most African cultures," Fuller said, "but I was impressed with Byang Kato's maturity, wisdom, intelligence, spirituality, and vision for Africa. That was the beginning of a close friendship."

Fuller thought Kato could become a professional journalist and offered to pay for his studies, but Kato felt that God was calling him to be a pastor.

The Atlantic Ocean at Lekki, near Lagos, Nigeria
© MATTHEW OMOJOLA | DREAMSTIME.COM

CHAPTER THREE

Student and Leader

Kato was convinced that the church in Africa needed well-trained pastors and teachers and that the education offered by most African Bible colleges was not sufficient. His goal was to study at a good school in Europe or America. But those schools required a certificate proving that his level of studies was equal to that of European or American students.

He studied hard to earn this certificate. Later that year he and his family moved back to Igbaja, where he could take a course that prepared students for the mandatory exam. After a while, Jummai, who was pregnant with their third child, returned to Kwoi, where Paul Sanom was born in October 1960.

Jummai found living apart from Byang challenging. "I was lonely," she said, "but I learned to have a closer walk with the Lord, as I had to train the children and manage the household affairs on my own."

After long days of study, Kato passed the exam and was invited to teach at a Bible school in Zabolo, about 120 miles northeast of Kwoi, where his family reunited. In the meantime, he applied to the London Bible College (LBC, today's London School of Theology).

He was surprised when LBC told him that they only accepted students who had passed the advanced level of the exam. Kato had passed the "ordinary" level. Angry and disappointed, he wanted to quit. He talked to different missionaries and to one of his previous pastors, looking for answers. "Actually, I tried everything but prayer," he said. When he finally turned over his problems to God, he found new courage to keep trying until he passed the advanced level.

London Bible College in the 1960s

Finally, in 1963, Byang was accepted by LBC and moved there for three years. Jummai joined him later, when he was halfway through his courses, leaving the children with some relatives. She arrived in December, when it was cold. "I complained about the weather and I missed the children," she said. But she believed it was important for her to be near her husband, even if he spent most of the day at school. She also took some classes. Knowing the challenges of being away from home, the couple opened their home to international students, especially those from Nigeria.

A close-up of Byang Kato and other students in the 1963 LBC photo

PROVIDED COURTESY OF LONDON SCHOOL OF THEOLOGY ©

Autumn

Back Row: D. Daniels, J. Angle, F. Ellis, D. Greengrass, B. Martin, R. Fry, D. Rees, G. Anstee, R. Haughton, O. Gay, D. Wells, P. Paine, I. Sinclair, C. Kounadis, G. Lee, N. McDonald, A. Taylor, C. Densham, R. Str...
Fourth Row: R. Martin, M. Bowerman, K. Wood, R. Johnston, R. Mussey, J. Hicks, Le Vinh Thach, F. Wright, S. Edwards, A. Eley, B. Harrison, R. Fung, P. Ball, K. Blackwell, R. Taylor, D. Johnson, A. Udonsak, E. Norman, E. Hall, A. Clark, A. Walker, R. Luhman, B. Stuart, C. Harding, B. Kato...
Third Row: R. Chester, S. Wilkinson, D. Burton, C. Clayton, M. Coles, H. Barlow, D. Jackson, J. Norris, N. Caplin, G. Andrews, E. Rowlands, J. Budd, W. Culling, W. Roberts, D. Mugford, P. Cambouropoulos, G. Larcombe, V. Reed, G. Turner, V. Dibble, G. Owen, J. Ndumbu, W. Phillips, R. Frith, P. Mort...
Second Row: R. Moore, A. Mason, E. Ritchie, K. McNeish, C. Cheung, R. Wilks, J. Preston, C. Woodhouse, C. Templar, A. Tear, E. Gulliver, R. Jones, D. Sander, P. Walford, M. Gurney, J. Peat, J. Paterson, B. Mugford, J. Fulcher, R. Berry, J. Webster, P. Symes, R. Vellacott, M. Peverall, S. Walker...
Front Row: C. Bristow, C. Kirk, J. Watts, S. Watson, M. Lough, V. Good, V. Farrow, V. Bristow, I. Glidden, M. Wickens, J. Lumb, V. Young, A. Long, D. Clark, M. Buss, J. Johnston, Rev. A. E. Cundall, Miss M. E. Manton, Mr. H. C. Oakley, Rev. J. Savage, Dr. R. P. Martin, Mr. H. H. Rowdon, Dr. H. ...

Kato found many opportunities to learn from both his professors and other students. The school's principal, Ernest Kevan, shared with the students his passion for the truths that had been uncovered during the Protestant Reformation of the sixteenth century and for the writings of Christians who had kept those truths alive.

The goal of the school was to prepare students for different callings in God's kingdom and to strengthen their understanding of the true teachings of the Bible at a time when some authors were challenging them. Along with other subjects, Hebrew and Greek were taught so that the students could read the Bible as it was originally written. The students also took the gospel to others, in London and other towns. During his first summer vacation, Kato and six other students preached the gospel around the county of Devon in southeast England.

1963.

G. Griffiths, B. Williams, R. Gemmell, T. Smith, P. Tout, D. Morris, D. Coomes, P. Smuts, J. Betts, A. Cleaton, A. Osuli, B. Powell, P. Lewis, C. Peat, R. Dewar, D. Adams, R. Lahey, K. Waddel, R. Hicks.
.d, R. Mayhew, H. Donaldson, D. Howells, S. Reading, A. Buxton, P. Hendry, R. Rogers, V. English, G. Mitchell, F. Evans, A. Berry, J. Risdon, W. Gould, M. Carnegie, C. Govier, R. Whitehouse, F. Churcher, R. Heywood, A. Higton, J. Thornton, M. Effa, R. Wigan, E. Holder, B. Aitken.
. Emery, J. Day, J. Summersby, J. Nicoll, K. Cheung P. Seccombe, R. Davey, M. Ryan, H. Hollanders, T. Withy, D. Barter, G. Parsons, E. Pickering, J. Blizzard, A. Ashton, A. Carruthers, A. Scott, R. Greig, R. Brockman, O. McDonald, M. Humfrey, S. Couch, B. Smith, E. Read, G. King, D. Bigg.
Upton, H. Keep, P. Jenkins, M. Endersbee, M. Noyce, E. McAllister, L. Calarge, H. Grainger, J. Gregory, S. Thorne, R. Gillbard, B. Fowler, M. Owen, H. McLees, M. Jones, N. Lockwood, A. Cater, M. Neville, M. Graham, K. Pusey, R. Singleton, N. Williams, D. Tyler, C. Prins, D. Cooper.
.ncipal, Rev. J. C. Connell, Dr. D. Guthrie, Mrs. M. J. Dannatt, Mr. L. C. Allen, Rev. O. J. Thomas, Mr. T. J. Buckley, S. Olyott, M. Nicolls, D. West, O. Guinness, R. Banks, E. Waller, E. Sayers, C. Dare, M. Anderson, W. Hill, G. Lloyd, C. Whitnee, F. Yeboah, H. Sorrell, E. Albarda, K. Scholz.

LBC's students and professors in 1963

PROVIDED COURTESY
OF LONDON SCHOOL OF
THEOLOGY ©

25

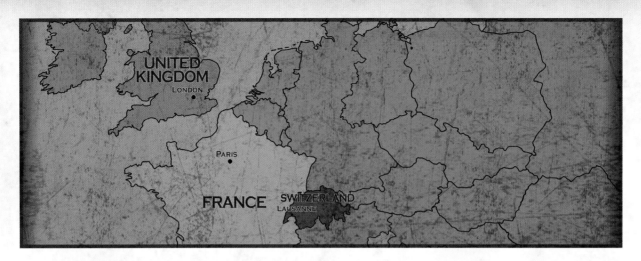

Map of England and France

TOM CARROLL

Kato graduated in 1966. Before returning to Nigeria, he and Jummai stopped at the European Bible Institute near Paris, France, to take a three-month course on how to teach the Bible to children, starting at a young age, both at home and in church.

After that Byang and Jummai put those teachings into practice with their own children, including them in the times of daily Bible reading and prayer they had established from the early days of their marriage. They also encouraged their children to ask questions at home so that they wouldn't have to look for answers somewhere else. "A child exposed to the Word of God at home is prepared for any atmosphere he will find in later life," Byang said.

Byang and Jummai encouraged other parents to do the same and to explain to their children what Jesus had done for sinners and why He is the only way to heaven. Soon, all three of the Kato children understood these important truths and placed their trust in Christ for their salvation.

Byang and Jummai Kato encouraged their children to study the Bible and to ask questions.

After that, Byang and Jummai moved to Igbaja, where Byang worked at the Bible college as a lecturer. They put everything they learned in France into practice.

In the meantime, Kato's abilities and training were being recognized. After spending some time training pastors at the Igbaja Seminary, he was chosen to be the general secretary of the Evangelical Church of West Africa (ECWA). It was an important position with great responsibilities, including the oversight of about twelve hundred churches.

Byang accepted the position and moved to ECWA's headquarters in Jos, almost one hundred miles northeast of Kwoi. The next year, he was ordained pastor of Bishara Church in the same town. The word *bishara* means "gospel" in Hausa. His parents, who had also become Christians, attended the church service.

The Kato family in 1963

PAUL KATO

The house where Kato lived while he was training pastors at the Igbaja Seminary

COURTESY OF REV. STEPHEN OLUWAROTIMI Y. BABA

Around the same time, Nigeria entered into a terrible war. It all started when the Igbo people of the southeast regions tried to form an independent state: the Republic of Biafra. The Nigerian government struck back, bombing cities, burning crops, and leaving the survivors homeless and starving. Even the area where Kato was born was affected by the fighting. Millions of people died before Biafra surrendered to Nigeria.

During the war, thousands of Biafrans looked for shelter in refugee camps.

Byang Kato checking cloth the church could use to produce clothes for the people of Biafra.
PAUL KATO

From the start ECWA organized programs to take assistance to those in need. They sent people to help at the only hospital in the area and provided truckloads of food for the people who were starving. In a country filled with so much anger and hatred, some donors were afraid that their gifts of food might fall into the wrong hands, but they trusted ECWA because the organization was honest.

ECWA also provided clothes for those who had lost everything in the war. To do so, they organized teams of tailors to work full-time on this project. They called this program Operation Dorcas, based on the name of a Christian mentioned in the Bible who made clothes for the needy (Acts 9:36–41). The Kato family had eight tailors working in their living room.

Kato had eight tailors working in his living room, making clothes
for the people who had lost everything in the war.

The packages of food and clothes were usually delivered by students from the Bible college, who also talked to the people and tried to bring them comfort. On each package, the students attached a paper with the promises of the gospel. Kato joined them a few times. Once, he preached to two thousand troops.

After the war ended in 1970, Kato realized that people needed tools to be able to grow their food again. He then started a new program called Operation Blacksmith, hiring local blacksmiths to make hoes and shovels that the students delivered to the people together with seeds and yams (a type of potato).

He also organized a meeting with all the ECWA pastors who had survived in the war-stricken areas and discussed how they and their people could be helped. After the meeting they all sang "Amazing Grace," praising the God who had kept them "through many dangers, toils, and snares."

Gwari women carrying African yams
in Abuja, the capital of Nigeria
JUJU FILMS

CHAPTER FOUR
For the African Church

In the meantime, Kato was still convinced that the African church needed better training. As more and more people became Christian, they needed pastors who could teach them the Bible correctly, studying it in its original languages and understanding what the church had learned in the past. When he mentioned it to George W. Peters, a professor from Dallas Theological Seminary (DTS) who was speaking in different parts of Africa, Peters convinced Kato to enroll in the seminary.

Kato was admitted to DTS in August 1970. He was the first African student there. Since the courses started in the fall, he spent the summer in Anchorage, Alaska, where he did mission work with Lake Spenard Baptist Church. During that time he gave over fifty talks and sermons. Living in Alaska was a new experience for Kato, who was especially surprised by the long nights.

Byang Kato with other missions faculty at Dallas Theological Seminary. He is second from the left, after George W. Peters. The two men at his right are George H. Houghton and Edwin C. Deibler.

COURTESY OF DALLAS THEOLOGICAL SEMINARY

Jummai joined him in Dallas a few months after he started his studies. Their children arrived some months later. Once the family was reunited, they hosted Good News Club meetings for their neighborhood children, following the guidelines Byang and Jummai had learned in France.

Deborah, John, and Paul were put in charge of knocking on doors and inviting children to their home. They were eager to do it, especially when they realized how many of these children didn't know Jesus. They found it surprising. They thought everyone in America was a Christian. They also helped their parents talk to the children who filled their living room.

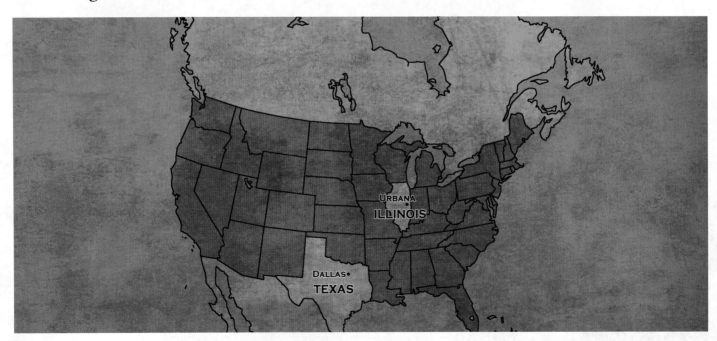

Map of North America

TOM CARROLL

Deborah, John, and Paul were in charge of knocking on doors and inviting children to their home.

Along with studying, Kato continued to tell others about the importance of missionary work. "I stand here as a living witness of what the Lord Christ Jesus has done through missions," he said to a group of 12,300 students who gathered in the small town of Urbana, Illinois, in 1970.

He had been invited to answer a specific question: "The National Church: Do They Want Us?" In other words, now that most churches in Africa, Asia, and Latin America had become independent of foreign help, did they still want missionaries from other continents? His answer was yes! He compared the large number of Africans who were turning to Jesus to the fish in a net that seemed almost too full to pull in. "We are beckoning to you to come and help us draw in the net," he said.

Some of the people attending the 1970 Urbana Student Missionary Convention
BUSWELL LIBRARY ARCHIVES & SPECIAL COLLECTIONS

He reminded the students that the church founded by Christ is universal. "The Lord Jesus Christ in the parable of the seeds (Matthew 13) pointed out that the world is the field," Kato said. "North America is just as needy as Africa, Asia and India. Christians of every race and color need the services of one another."

Even Christians who went to Africa for work or as tourists could help to build the kingdom of God there, Kato said, just by being good examples, being ready to answer questions about their faith, and encouraging people to attend local churches. In fact, they "can often go where personnel under missionary societies may not be welcome."

Kato speaking at the Urbana Student Missionary Convention

BUSWELL LIBRARY ARCHIVES & SPECIAL COLLECTIONS

Kato repeated this teaching of one church under Christ in a paper he wrote when he graduated from DTS. He later published it as *Theological Pitfalls in Africa*. It was a good title. A pitfall is a type of trap that people cannot see. Kato wanted to warn the African churches about some serious dangers few people had yet noticed.

One pitfall was the temptation to find unity in national traditions instead of finding it in Christ. Kato was concerned about some teachers who said that African religions are so similar to Christianity that anyone could be saved without the Bible and without Christ just by following their traditions and living a good life. That's not possible, Kato said, because only "he who has the Son has life" (1 John 5:12), and no one can know God's Son without the Bible, where He has chosen to reveal Himself.

Kato had a deep appreciation of African culture. He also knew that some of the greatest men and women of the early church, such as Augustine of Hippo, Athanasius, Tertullian, Perpetua, and Felicita, were born in Africa. But these people were moved by the same gospel that moved Christians in other parts of the world, and their writings were meant to inspire people all over the world, not just in Africa.

Kato's seminary course was supposed to last two years, but he finished in one, graduating with honors in 1971. He then studied two more years to earn a higher degree. In the end he was given the Four Way Test Award, which was granted to the student who seemed most consistent in his Christian life and had the most potential for becoming a good leader. Kato saw it as a huge honor but said that his deepest desire was to bring glory to God.

Kato during his last year at DTS
COURTESY OF DALLAS THEOLOGICAL SEMINARY

A few months before finishing his studies, Kato was invited to a conference about Christian education in Limuru, Kenya. Before leaving his family, he prayed for safety and asked the children if they knew that whatever happened to any of them, they were all safe in Christ. When the children said yes, he asked them to show him some Bible verses that proved what they believed. They quoted John 1:12 and John 14:6. This gave Kato peace of mind.

His message at the conference was so clear and powerful that the leaders of the Association of Evangelicals in Africa and Madagascar (AEAM) who had organized the conference wondered if God had finally answered their prayers.

For almost three years, they had been looking for someone with the same concerns as Kato and with a high level of education, someone who could stand at the same level as many university professors who believed that the gospel could change from place to place and that all religions led to God. They were also looking for someone who could help them build more Christian colleges and schools in Africa. While they were looking, Kato was in America, preparing for exactly that position. It was a perfect match.

Kato's nomination as general secretary of AEAM was confirmed during a meeting. Kato was asked to leave the room during the vote. When he returned, everyone rose in his honor, giving thanks to God. They had all voted yes.

When Kato returned to the room, everyone rose in his honor.

It was a great responsibility because the association covered the whole continent of Africa. To fill the position, the Kato family had to move to Nairobi, the capital of Kenya, which was fast becoming one of the most modern cities in the world. There, they became members of the Nairobi Baptist Church.

Byang prayed that God would give him the needed wisdom and strength to perform all of his new duties: organizing, writing, speaking, and publishing. He also prayed for Jummai, who would have to take on many responsibilities by herself, especially during his frequent travels. Everywhere he went, he continued to share the gospel with anyone he met, including those who sat next to him on his many airplane flights. Those who knew him described him as warm, humble, and friendly.

Kato supervised the production of papers, booklets, posters, and cassette tapes that could spread the pure message of the gospel all over Africa.

PAUL KATO

Kato shared the gospel with everyone he met.

Not everyone liked Kato's writings. Some Africans still thought of Christianity as a religion for White people, so when Kato told them to put the Bible before their traditions, they thought he was promoting a European or American culture.

Once, when the editor of a religious newspaper came to visit him, Kato talked to him freely about his desire to help every Christian in Africa know the Bible better and follow it more closely. He thought the interview went well. The next day, he was shocked to discover that the editor had published a front-page article attacking both him and AEAM.

Kato was sad and disappointed. He suffered many sleepless nights. Finally, his family and friends helped him to see that no matter what other people said, putting the Bible first was always the right thing to do.

Kato was shocked to discover that an editor he had trusted attacked him in a front-page article.

Kato tried to explain over and over what he meant. The problem was that some people read only one or two of his papers and didn't get a clear idea of what he was saying. He understood that many things should be adapted from culture to culture. For example, many churches in Europe and North America use pianos or organs to help people sing in tune, but those instruments are not necessary. Kato said that in Africa, Christians can also use African instruments, keeping "in mind, of course, that the sound of music must not drown out the message."

Children keeping the beat at a church in Nigeria
MARIEKE UDE-DEN HOLLANDER

"Christians should remain Africans wherever their culture does not conflict with the Bible," he said. They could keep traditional clothes, local styles of music, and many customs, as long as these things didn't contradict the Bible. Otherwise, "it's the Bible that must judge the culture."

One example of problems with traditional religions was seen in the country of Chad, in central Africa. Eager to emphasize local customs, the government of Chad revived the practice of initiation, similar to the one Kato experienced when he was young.

If this had been just a cultural tradition, Kato said, Christians would have been glad to participate. Teaching young people to be brave and tough is a good thing. But the initiation in Chad included a pledge of allegiance to the traditional gods, calls to the spirits of the dead, and acts of violence—all things that Christians could not do. Because of their refusal to participate in these practices, some churches had been closed and some Christians, including pastors, had been tortured and killed.

When Kato traveled to Chad to talk to pastors, he realized that to stand strong under persecution, many Christians needed a better understanding of the true meaning of Christianity. If it's just a collection of teachings on how to be good people, as some thought, it would not be different from any other religion, and pledging allegiance to a foreign god would not be causing major problems. But Christianity is something completely different.

To provide better training for pastors who would later teach the people in their area, Kato promoted the building of a seminary in Bangui, the capital of the Central African Republic, which Christians from that part of Africa could attend. This was the first seminary in French-speaking Africa.

He also wrote a letter to encourage all Christians to pray for Chad, reminding them that "the future for the church in Chad is as bright as our Lord's promise in Matthew 16:18"—the powers of hell will never be able to defeat it.

This building of the Bangui Evangelical School of Theology houses the chapel and library.
COURTESY OF DAVID SPRINGER

In the meantime, Kato's responsibilities continued to grow. One event followed another, giving him hardly any time to rest. Nairobi was known as "the Crossroads of Africa" because many people from all over the continent met there. Besides speaking at different conferences, Kato opened his house to many of the people who attended them. He also spoke at the local university and was interviewed by magazines and radio stations.

At a conference in Lausanne, Switzerland, he explained that he had the same passion as Robert Moffat, a Scottish nineteenth-century missionary who had said, "If I had a thousand lives, I would give them to the service of Christ in Africa." At times it seemed that Kato really had a thousand lives because he did so much more than most people. At the same conference, he also reminded Christians that those who proclaimed that Christ is the only way of salvation would never be popular.

Byang Kato and other Christians at a meeting, with the AEAM building behind them

PAUL KATO

Kato's position took him all over the world. His favorite trip, however, was the one he took back to his hometown, where he spoke in a packed church. He also played a recording of his wife and children sending their love to all. In the afternoon, he borrowed a bicycle and went all over town visiting old friends.

But these times of fun and relaxation were becoming rare. Around the end of 1975, while he was planning a trip that would take him away from home for three months, Byang decided to plan a vacation with Jummai and his children at a sea resort near Mombasa, about 150 miles southeast of Nairobi.

A street in Kwoi
PAUL KATO

When Kato visited his hometown, he borrowed a bicycle and went all over town visiting old friends.

CHAPTER FIVE
Leaving a Powerful Message

Byang, Jummai, and their boys left for their vacation on December 16. Deborah went to Nigeria instead to represent her family at a family reunion. Three days later, on Jonathan's birthday, Byang gave his son a gift of money to put in the bank, then took the boys to town, where he gave Paul a driving lesson.

They ended their morning by walking on the beach near the place they were renting. The tide was low, so they waded in the water to explore a coral reef. Just before lunchtime, the boys became hungry, and Byang told them they could go back to their place. He was going to join them soon, he said.

A view of Mombasa, Kenya

HENRI BERGIUS, FLICKR

Kato and his sons spent time together at the beach near the place they were renting.

The boys helped their mother make lunch. When Byang didn't show up, they thought he was talking to someone on the beach. But when the one o'clock news came on, they started to be concerned. "Where's Baba?" Jonathan asked. "He never misses the one o'clock news."

They looked for him on the beach but could not find him. They called some neighbors, as well as the police. A search went on until midnight, when the sky turned too dark to see anything. Jummai and the boys could hardly sleep.

The next day they received some sad news. Kato's body was found in the morning. He had drowned. No one knew exactly what happened. He knew how to swim and didn't have any marks on his skin that suggested a poisonous fish might have stung him. Some people wondered if he had swum too far and become too exhausted to swim back.

Byang Kato's family and friends held a memorial service for him in Nairobi, then flew his body to Kwoi, where it was buried on December 24. The Boys' and Girls' Brigades formed a line along the street that led to the local church. About twelve hundred people attended the service inside, and many more sat and stood outside. In the meantime, memorial services were held in other places, and many Christians sent letters of condolences to the Kato family.

Francis Schaeffer, a famous pastor from Switzerland, wrote his reaction to the news of Kato's death: "I literally wept. The loss for Africa and the Lord's work seemed so great."

Harold Fuller, the editor of *African Challenge* who had been a friend of Kato since they first met, wondered why, of all people, God had to take Byang Kato, who had just begun to bring great improvements to the African church.

But God always knows what He is doing and has not abandoned the church in Africa. What Kato did in his short life was like a seed that continued to grow. Since then, AEAM has created many programs to train new leaders and has issued many new publications, emphasizing the same gospel that Kato held high.

At a time when many people in Africa were wondering if their identity as Africans had been lost under centuries of European rule, Kato reminded Christians their true identity was in Christ. This message proved to be important not only in Africa but all over the world, where Kato's writings are just beginning to be appreciated.

Kato had always hoped that today's Africans would one day become leaders for the entire Christian world, just as the early Christians of North Africa had been for their generation. He might just be one of the first of this new group of Christian forerunners.

Time Line of Kato's Life

1936 – Byang Kato is born in Sabzuro, in the district of Kwoi, Nigeria.

1946 – Kato goes through the traditional initiation that marked the passage from boy to man. He later hears the gospel from a Christian teacher.

1948 – Kato is baptized and adopts Henry as his middle name.

1953 – During a revival, Kato devotes his life to Christ.

1955 – He is admitted to the Bible college in Igbaja.

1957, *January* – He marries Jummai Rahila.

November – Their first child, Deborah Bosede, is born.

December – Kato graduates from Bible college and returns to Kwoi.

1958 – He serves in a counseling ministry at the *African Challenge* magazine.

December – The Katos' second child, Jonathan Nzuno, is born.

1960 – Kato moves back to Igbaja for further studies.

October – Their third child, Paul Sanom, is born.

1963 – Kato moves to England to attend LBC.

1964 – Jummai joins him in London.

1966 – Kato graduates from LBC. He and Jummai attend a three-month course in France to learn how to teach the Bible to children.

1967 – Start of the Nigerian civil war. Kato becomes general secretary of the ECWA.

1968 – Kato is ordained to be a pastor.

1970 – Kato serves with Lake Spenard Baptist Church in Anchorage, Alaska, then enters DTS in Texas.

1971 – First Jummai, then their children arrive in Dallas. The family starts a Good News Club.

1973 – Kato is appointed general secretary of the AEAM. He assumes the position soon after graduating from DTS and moves to Nairobi, Kenya, with his family.

1975 – He dies in Mombasa, Kenya.

Did you know?

Africa is the second-largest continent in the world. It's made up of fifty-four countries with about 1.2 billion people. Most of these countries are very different from each other. Nigeria, with over 206 million people, has the largest population in Africa, and its main commercial center, Lagos, is the largest on the continent. The people of Nigeria include about 250 different groups with different languages and cultures. The main groups are the Hausa, the Igbo, and the Yoruba. Nigeria was one of the seventeen countries that declared its independence in 1960. It had officially been under British rule since 1901.

In the area around Kwoi, archaeologists have found some interesting sculptures made by the Nok culture, one of the earliest-known societies of Western Africa (from around 500 BC to AD 200). Most of the sculptures are in terra cotta (fired clay), but many objects show that the Nok were also masters at using iron and bronze. The sculptures are very refined and realistic and follow some definite artistic rules. The rich clothes and jewels portrayed on the images of kings give an idea of the wealth of some African kingdoms. In one of his writings, Kato said, "I was amazed at the great similarity I saw between the terra cotta unearthed in Israel and the ones found at Nok, which is only four miles from my home. Did some great civilization flourish in the Sudan and perish?"

Some of the richest kingdoms in the world were in Africa. Most people know only about the Egyptian Empire, but the Kanem Empire (covering part of Niger, Cameroon, Chad, and Nigeria) was also very powerful when it was defeated by Islamic armies in 1090. The

Mali Empire (larger than the present Mali Republic) reached the height of its power in the fourteenth century under Mansa Musa. In the sixteenth century, Europe was amazed at the riches and high culture of the Songhai Kingdom of Sudan. Another impressive African kingdom around the same time was the Kingdom of Benin in the southwest of Nigeria (not to be confused with the modern-day country Benin, formerly called Dahomey).

❧ In the Hausa language, the word Kaduna (the name of the state where Kato was born) means "crocodile." The state was given this name because there were many crocodiles in the Kaduna River.

❧ Some farmers in Kwoi grow a special type of rice known as acha, fonio, or hungry rice. High in protein and iron, it's a favorite among locals. Since it is less common than other types of rice, it is usually kept for special occasions. It's often part of the customary presents a man in Nigeria gives to the family of the woman he wants to marry.

❧ Some of the foods the Kato family considered essential were corn, palm oil, sweet potatoes, and yams. Palm oil is made from the fruit (or nuts) of oil palm trees. The same fruit is ground into a paste and used to make a tasty soup that is popular in Nigeria and in other West African countries. Peanut butter (known as groundnut paste) is also used to make a similar soup.

This soup can be eaten with rice or with fufu, a dough made with plantains, sweet potatoes, taros, or cassava (or a combination of these), which are first boiled and then pounded together in a large mortar. Usually one person pounds the vegetables in the mortar with a long pestle while another person turns the dough. Fufu is eaten with clean hands to scoop up the soup.

For snacks, many people buy food from street vendors. Some popular Nigerian snacks are roasted plaintain with roasted peanuts;

fried plantain, potato, or yam; popcorn and roasted peanuts; and roasted corn. Some vendors peel oranges and cut off the top so that people can squeeze them and drink the juice while they are walking. Another favorite drink with children is cashew fruit juice (from the fruit that holds the nut we normally buy).

According to Byang's son Paul, Byang's favorite dish was rice with chicken or beef in a tomato sauce. This was a treat when Byang was growing up. Typical food would be tuwo acha, gwaza, and yams with little to no meat because meat was reserved for special occasions. As an adult, Byang said he had an "international stomach" because he loved diversity in food.

❧ Most Christians in Africa use native musical instruments during worship. Drums and other percussion instruments are especially common, as they help to keep the rhythm. People also clap and move at the beat of each song.

❧ Soccer is a very popular sport in Africa. Byang loved to play soccer. Unlike his sons, he was not very good at it, but they still had fun playing together.

❧ Nigerians are used to carrying things on their head. They start learning this when they are children. By the time they are older, they can carry even large and heavy objects without holding them with their hands.

❧ Coral reefs look like groups of colorful rocks underwater. In reality, they are made out of thousands of living creatures called polyps, which group together to survive. When the polyps die, they leave their skeleton structures, which become the building structure of coral reefs. Coral reefs come in many shapes and colors and provide food and shelter to fish and other sea animals.

❀ In the Kato family picture on page 28, you can see some typical African clothes and hats. Often African clothes are very colorful. Many women wrap colorful cloth around their bodies and around their heads. Men wear many types of traditional caps.

❀ In Dallas the Kato children attended a private school called Trinity Christian Academy. "We were the only Black kids in the school," Paul Kato said, "but we had no problems at all because we were very athletic and we knew it was a privilege to attend the school. We also did not have a problem because of the support we had from home and the knowledge we were loved. How my dad could afford to send us there I don't know, because we lived in a poor area of Dallas. But his belief in a good education for his kids was second to none."

❀ Jummai played a great part in Byang's work. Along with taking care of the children and other family responsibilities while Byang was gone, she was his main proofreader and typist. According to her son Paul, she "never complained and always took one day at a time." After Byang's death, it was hard for her to make ends meet, but she made sure the children continued to attend excellent schools. When Jonathan and Paul were almost expelled from Spring Arbor University in Michigan for lack of funds, she went with tears in her eyes to beg the missionary board for help (which they gave). Later, her children supported her in her old age. She died in her sleep on May 9, 2019.

From the Pen of Byang Kato

The inspired, inerrant Word of God gives us the gospel and its working power in a nutshell in 1 Corinthians 15:1–4. It is not a part of any people's culture….The Jews did not have it. The Germans, the Americans, the Africans, the Europeans needed to get it revealed through a messenger (Romans 10:9, 10). The gospel must be received….All men, therefore, regardless of their ethnic origin are entirely helpless, in fact, spiritually dead (Ephesians 2:1; Romans 5:6).

The Christian faith is not a leap in the dark. When I say I believe, the sentence is meaningless unless I give the object of my belief. The centre of the gospel…is not the cosmic Christ present in all religious aspirations of various faiths in the world. It is a historic person, Jesus the Christ. That He lived and died under Pontius Pilate is verifiable. That He was buried and literally rose again is also a convincing fact of history. A long list of His contemporaries who saw Him after resurrection was unchallenged. The best the religious leaders could do was to bribe the guards to conceal the truth (Matthew 28:11–15). No amount of fraud can destroy the truth of God predicted several millennia earlier. That Jesus died, was buried and rose again is not only an undisputable fact of history, but it is a fact borne out in the lives of more than half a billion people in the world today. He alone as God-man has made the claims of death, resurrection and a promise of drawing men to Himself, and the claims have been fulfilled. This is the undiluted gospel for which Christ's sons and daughters in Africa must be prepared to lay down their lives (Matthew 10:34–39).

Christianity is unique. It creates the new race, a race called "the body of Christ," made up of people from any cultural background.

The days of persecution for the Bible-believing Christian may not be too far away. Christians all over the world should pray for more grace for the third world followers and heralds of the unique Christ. Meanwhile the Bible-believing Christian should respect and pray "for kings and all who are in high positions, that we may lead a quiet and peaceable life, godly and respectful in every way" (1 Timothy 2:2 RSV). Christians in Africa should realize that to stand for the uniqueness of Christ will not be popular as ungodliness increases in the world. There may come a time when Christians will have to say, "For we cannot but speak the things which we have seen and heard" (Acts 4:20). They may even have to say, "We ought to obey God rather than men" (Acts 5:29) and face the consequences that Stephen and others after him faced.

Acknowledgments

I started this book with little information about Kato and little hope of finding photos. To my amazement, one contact has led to another, until I was surrounded by wonderful people willing to provide me with documents, photos, and suggestions.

I was first introduced to Kato by Marieke Ude-Den Hollander, counselor at John Calvin Secondary School in Oswanka and wife of the local pastor and school principal, Rev. Nicodemus Ude. Marieke has also encouraged me throughout the writing process and has given me much valuable advice.

The first person to provide documents and addresses was Rev. Dr. David K. Tarus, executive director of ACTEA (Association for Christian Theological Education in Africa), who has read this manuscript and sent me dozens of files with Kato's speeches and writings.

I especially owe a large debt of gratitude to Paul Kato, son of Byang Kato and founder and CEO of Kato International Training Academy in Kwoi, Nigeria, who has read my manuscript, sent me some excellent photos, and generously answered my numerous questions.

I am also grateful to Rev. Dr. S. J. Garland, international director-at-large of Africa Christian Textbooks, for his suggestions and encouragement; to Rev. Stephen Oluwarotimi Y. Baba, professor of biblical studies and former provost/president of ECWA Theological Seminary and former provost/president of ECWA College of Education, Igbaja, for providing valuable photos and information; to Blaize Itodo, a journalist, artist, and photographer in Abuja, Nigeria, who has provided much information about his beautiful and ancient country; and to others who have chosen to remain anonymous.

As always, I am grateful to my husband, Tom, for his constant encouragement and patience; to my exceptional artist, Matt Abraxas; and to Dr. Joel Beeke, David Woollin, Jay Collier, Annette Gysen, and all the staff at Reformation Heritage Books (RHB) for their continued vision and support. Publishing a book about a man who is still fairly unknown outside of Africa has taken courage and has shown once again that RHB is unique in its priorities and motives.